in the garden

In this book, Miriel Lenore draws on her skills as storyteller and delves into myth, lore, science and history to evoke the life of a great garden, the Adelaide Botanic Garden.

Miriel Lenore was born in Boort, Victoria, and was educated there and in Bendigo and Melbourne. She worked as a plant breeder and student counsellor before moving to Fiji where she was involved in adult education as well as teaching in schools. After twenty-two years there, and a brief period in Sydney, she moved to Adelaide where she still lives.

Also by Miriel Lenore

in the garden

Miriel Lenore

Wakefield Press

Wakefield Press
1 The Parade West
Kent Town
South Australia 5067
www.wakefieldpress.com.au

First published 2007

Designed by Liz Nicholson, designBITE
Cover photographs: Sophie Abbott — namaskara@optusnet.com.au
Section photographs: Sophie Abbott, Ruth Raintree and Mick Bradley
Typeset by Clinton Ellicott, Wakefield Press
Printed and Bound by Hyde Park Press

National Library of Australia
Cataloguing-in-publication entry

Lenore, Miriel.
In the garden.

ISBN 978 1 86254 751 3 (pbk.).

1. Gardens — Poetry. I. Title.

A821.3

Government of South Australia
Arts SA

seed leaf flour frute

herbe, bee and tree

are more than I may sing

Nicholas Grimald (16th C)

The worst of gardening, said Mrs Miniver, . . .

is that it's so full of metaphors one hardly

knows where to begin

Jan Struther

for
Alana Adele

List of poems

※

※

Gardens are not made by singing

Rudyard Kipling

To make a botanic garden

Was Queen Hatshepsut
sending to Punt for incense trees
the first botanic gardener?

Collectors persist —
heedless of dysentery
malaria, broken legs and death
cases of seeds and specimens
cross alps and oceans:

> cannas from Turkey
> peonies from Japan
> cedars from Lebanon
> Hawaiian hibiscus
> proteas from Africa

Classifying botanists then arrive
and gardeners on small tractors
with carts of cuttings and tools
the makers of ponds and fountains
a politician needing a monument

Add lovers of beauty and oddity
kissing couples and tired shoppers
hospital patients in wheelchairs
birthday parties and weddings
Chinese students from Harbin

In the Garden

the summers of Hesperides are long
     Emily Dickinson

Gardens began in the desert
with tired and thirsty men
wanting water, shade and fruit

After the bustle of Rundle Mall
I relax eating grapes
under the giant fig above the lake .
in this Garden I share with the city.
I'm reminded of those Persian nobles
        who kept the desert at bay
with high walls and a sense of order
those Hebrews for whom Eden meant
        garden of delight

Memories grow like the grass I lie on:
bananas and waterlilies
            on the banks of the Rewa
the claret ash at Leaghur
Hilgay's lime avenue, Buxted's yew
the River Reds of Lake Boort

An apartment dweller with pots
            of geranium and basil
my sacred garden is here with lotus
            plum and bamboo
testament to beauty in simplicity, in age
            even in blemish

That *ripeness is all* appeals more
                as the years mount:
Hesperides summers *are* blissfully long
my thoughts float, the grapes disappear
a boy chasing ducks turns to stroke
                the velvet of a salvia

Systematics

If bringing order from chaos
is the Creator's finest task
Carolus Linnaeus saw himself
as a second Adam
marshalling plants
into their Kingdom of Divisions
Classes Orders Families
Genera and Species

The Father of Systematic Botany
knew appearances deceive
inner depths distinguish —
ovules and pollen grains
rank the humble daisy
above the majestic conifer

Botany was his *beloved science*
sexual classification *the Ariadne thread*.
surrounded by plants in their classes
his satisfied bust rises from the daisies

Post-colonial

Wisteria begins its yearly
cascade from the arch
looks settled here

London plane trees
(*Platanus hybrida, origin unknown*)
wear delicate new leaves

The rhetorical oak
clumsy with years and surgery
stands centre stage

A man in shirtsleeves
rakes the path: it could be
London in the better parts

Kensington Gardens perhaps
though our Peter Pan
was stolen years ago

Kensington's now Arabia
while Australians born in Italy
and Vietnam picnic on this lawn

Birthday

for Rosalie

Late autumn in the Garden
no crowds
no riot of colours
the beds are resting

Only the odd callistemon in flower
and one exuberant *Hakea*
defying winter with its
                jaunty declaration
as you my friend who loves this place
whose bright spirit dares
                a flagging body

You dance to mountain flutes
                on your 83rd birthday
read philosophy and poetry
                through a magnifying glass
write letters to a world
                that *does* write back

Surrounded by blossoms
we have shared a thermos at this table
talking of eternity
                    laughing at the ducks

You ever notice that trees do everything to git attention that we do, except walk?

Alice Walker

Petrified tree

Thirty-five million years ago
greened
by a northern sun
it sheltered the first pigeons

Fallen into a lake
and coated
with crystals
wood turned to stone

Sent from Vienna
to celebrate
the Garden's birth
and planted here as if to grow

it's a polished landing ground
for butterflies
(life span two months)
opening bright wings to the sun

Our royal palm

planted by Duchess of York (Queen Mary) July 1901

Among palms from Laos and Queensland
the Chilean wine palm *Jubaea chilensis*
faces the main gate, upright and stately
like the Duchess soon to be Queen

who planted it as the Commonwealth began.
Was it named for Juba

                ancient King of Mauretania
or from the slaves' word for a freedom
the Duchess was seldom to know?

The Duke was too ill to plant
the companion palm across the path
A local eminence wielded the shovel
resulting in a smaller plainer tree

Secure in the burnished glory of its inner spathe
the pockmarked trunk lifts lively fronds
to hearten patients at the windows
of the hospital's Oncology Ward

13

The living fossil

Once animals were captive
in the centre of the Garden
now a pine tree is behind bars

Found in the Greater Blue Mountains
the precious *Wollami nobilis* stands
in its cage on the slope above the lake

Known only from fossils till 1994
rarity and phylogeny combine
to make this a remarkable plant

Not named for its character, Gondwana's
forgotten pine honours David Noble
the Park Ranger who found it

Healthy after its transplanting here
it will test, with a Mount Lofty sibling
the effects of habitat

A child puts his fingers through the bars
the pine does not bite

Errata

Below are the notes with correct page references.

p 15 Hallam, Lord Tennyson, was Governor of South Australia and later Governor General of Australia. He was the first child of the poet who named him after his great friend Arthur Henry Hallam, for whom he wrote the elegy, In Memoriam.

p 52 The proverb, Good wine needs no bush, goes back to Roman times when ivy bushes (sacred to Bacchus) were used to advertise taverns and wine sellers.

p 55 'The trio of pine, plum and bamboo, known as the three friends of winter, was indispensable in a Chinese garden.' Richard Aitken: Botanical Riches.

p 71 The poet was Francis Webb.

The oak

Branches of the huge Burr Oak
(*Quercus macrocarpa — East North America*)
touch the ground on three sides
the fourth is cut away
for us to sip tea at white plastic tables

Those plebian birds (or so I think)
black ducks and seagulls pick up crumbs
but the tree is *noble*:

Planted by the State's Governor in 1901
            Hallam, Lord Tennyson
who carried always (did his mother agree?)
his father's love for his friend

reminding me that poetry, love and iced coffee
            are the centre of my city

Aphrodite's golden apple

Cydonia oblonga

I pictured the apple Paris gave
as a precious artefact
or a *sunkissed* Golden Delicious

never a mundane quince —
difficult to peel
the fruit acidic and tough

So unromantic
hardly grand enough
to distract Atalanta

or to need a dragon guard
in the Hesperides' paradise
at the end of the world

Yet this is the fruit still
thrown into the bridal carriage
eaten at wedding feasts.

Espaliered against the café wall
branches stretched along wires were
gently trained to increase bearing
:
That discipline fosters fruitfulness
today's Dionysians
don't wish to contemplate

The white goddess

Prunus persica, flowering peach

Planted twelve years ago by
our Premier and Okayama's Governor
to grow friendship between two different
                    and distant lands

So insignificant in winter with patches
of yellow lichen on its few skinny sticks
beside slender Mexican palms
                    and robust pines

Then buds at the end of twigs swell to leaves
bare branches covered with a host
of double white blossoms offer
          their annual ecstasy to bees

Seen from a distance the sun has turned it
into the white cloak of a goddess
the grassed slope behind her the stage
                    for some ritual act

Anatolia's White Goddess of corn and honey
adds peach to her portfolio
ancient mother of states and people, she may
                    even bring us peace

Pepper tree

Schinus molle var. areira, planted 1863

Fed on night soil in its early years
survivor of recurrent surgery
knotted, misshapen giant
      a huge bustle at its back
the pepper tree towers over the entrance
takes me back to the Mallee

Coconut palm of the dry lands
often a farm's only garden
      it had to find hidden water
sticky leaves could waste none
kept north-west dust from the house
branches were climbing frames and castles
the pink peppercorns *ammo* for peashooters
      in kids' perpetual wars

In this Garden where sprinklers are turning
                        beside the Lotus pool
the mallee section features acacia and eucalypts
                        but there are no pepper trees

Favourites

What is your favourite tree in the Garden?
Impossible to answer the child's question

A Eucalypt perhaps, a *rubida*, *citriodora*
or the pre-contact River Red on the lawn

Sometimes it's the crocodile-skin bark
of the towering Red Cedar

or a survivor like the twisted Mallee
with crimson flowers and huge fruits

the bottle shaped *Brachychiton*
promising more than it gives

the layered Himalayan cedar
the Indians call *wood of the gods*

its neighbouring Araucaria with
chimney-sweep top brushing the sky

Not likely to be a dedicated tree
chosen less for beauty than purpose:

to remember nurses, a visiting Queen
Soroptimists and Governors

though the flame tree honouring
a past director manages both

Arbutus

Some days my favourite tree
is the arbutus:
the twisted horizontal limbs
of the American species
propped against age
Canary Islands saplings' russet bark
lighting up the lawn
and especially the Irish strawberry
Arbutus unedo

Bunches of today's tiny white bells
will become the summer fruits
of its common name
giving us an Italian liqueur yet
unedo (I eat but once) is proof
beauty and taste are not always kin

The trunk in any season grips attention
the geometrical jigsaw dries to
strips of curling bark ready to fall
smooth powdery limbs catch
the sun in shades of salmon
orange-pink, just a hint of green

Firewheel tree

Stenocarpus sinuatus

Red and yellow whorls
shimmy up and down
the gigantic tree
join earth to heaven:

martyred St Catherine
on her fiery wheel
goes home
on Jacob's ladder

This tree
says Margaret Preston
to me
but
doesn't know
that it's art

Sappho

Rhododendron 'Sappho'

*Shiver when Sappho speaks of her Heart Beat. It
Pounding down through the ages*
          Eileen Myles

Shiver at this world
of dramatic blossoms:
dark eyes in white faces
inky flares at each heart

Strangers debate the colour
cerise crimson claret ruby?
devotees together
now become friends for life

Did a scholar name this marvel
to honour Plato's tenth muse
knowing her passion
for flowers as well as girls?

She who wrote: *Dead,*
I won't be forgotten.

Memorial

Planted twenty years ago
                    by General Eva Burrows
the thin and twisted gum
hardly suggests those muscular
                    Christians it celebrates

They beat the drum here in 1880 to begin
Australia's Salvation Army
maintain the tradition that would save
                    soul *and* body:
whoever hasn't eaten today
                    come to my house

The tree's sparse foliage and scrawny limbs
bear witness to hard times
                    but it too has survived

Having known it as *Eucalyptus citriodora*
I resist its move to the *Corymbia* genus
                    however time etc
perhaps today's Salvationists may find
a more pacific name for their cause

Adelaide's own

Fraxinus rotundifolia ssp oxycarpa 'Raywood'

Once a random mutation
    in an Adelaide nursery
now planted over half the world
the claret ash in Botanic Park
    bears historic scars

No longer slim and elegant
with every leaf an autumn gem
it holds the large well-rounded shape
of bibulous drinkers in their later years

Though the high branches still flaunt
their rich breath-catching merlot
lower leaves remain green or the dun
colour of Penfolds Grange left
    too long to drink

I gave my mother a claret ash
when, in her fifties, unwillingly
she followed my father to his farm
carried water in buckets
                to begin a garden

Rare to find such subtle colour beside
the black box and Murray pine
of the Loddon floodplains
Thirty years after her death
the ash still decorates
        the abandoned garden
and the heroic display in Botanic Park
                gives her back to me

Evergreens

Where Dell Bridge spans First Creek
an English yew
        and Californian redwood
           are neighbours

Hecate's tree, Robin's longbow:
Taxus baccata
        the yew named by the Greeks
for its bow wood or its poison,
glum watcher at the Battle of the Gods
           protector from evil
and renewing itself from decay
this tree is a baby to its English relatives
        growing since the Bronze Age

All living things were made under a redwood
           the Tolana say
These guardians of streams
           will live for ever
unless killed by gales or lightning
        the forest guides assure you

Though one tree in California is
       the largest living thing on earth
this specimen is not so tall but thin
                  anorexic even
dead patches in the tight green cloak
belie its confident name
       Sequoia sempervirens

In this place on this day I feel no envy
though my lifespan is nearer to
       the lilies of the field

**Ensnared with flowers,
I fall on grass**

Andrew Marvell

Bailey's Triangle

Hard not to say *riot of colour*
at first sight of those giant dahlias
staring above the hedge of holly-oak

Yellow red white maroon and purple petals
(only blue is absent) form seventeen
types of head — single and double
pompoms miniatures whorls and spikes
the monsters nod —

                too big to stay erect

Dowdy amongst the kaleidoscope
I'm at home with stylish Betty
Mattie Christie Simone and Pam
Vera Barbara Sally and Miss Joan

                all tagged around me

At the centre of this rainbow
an Englishman from the south of France
(black felt hat banded with tiny shells)
studies the dull grey pigeon
                    scrabbling at our feet
his first words to me: *what bird is that?*

Herb circles

Furious when the roses were
banished from their circular beds
around the cherub's fountain

I now love purple loosestrife
swallowort, knitbone, heal-all
feverfew and nosebleed
lad's love, bouncing Bet
horse-heal and kiss me quick

With right use they will cure the plague
deter vampires witches and fleas
put money in our pockets
protect us from lightning strikes
grow hair on our chins and make
pigeons and straying husbands come home

How can we ever be ill with such herbs
to heal our blindness hysteria
arthritis fevers and indigestion?
our toothache wounds and dysentery
our colic rheumatism cramps
and the bite of mad dogs?

Euphorbia

Euphorbia n: spurge, exuding an acrid milky
*   substance with purgative properties*
spurge v:. cleanse, purify, clear of guilt
        Shorter Oxford Dictionary

It is September 11

She's been coming for years
to this Classground where plants
line up in their Families:
here there are always flowers

Today she is incensed:
two trees have been badly pruned
we've lost the Glenelg foreshore to greed
now Gardens money is spent on freeways
and staff are cut

This tough desert *Euphorbia* —
splashes of blood above its fierce thorns —
was her first pot plant at eight
I was heartbroken when my father took it
for his own

The green flowers of another *Euphorbia*
stand out above bracts like eyeballs on stalks
she sees coffee cups on a tray

She talks of her garden — its birds and beetles
the little animals scrabbling among the plants
the delight of helping things live

Sacred papyrus

Spider legs fly-whisks or untidy coronets
the delicate heads of *Cyperus papyrus*
wave above insouciant green stalks
wearing their importance lightly

The dry square beds of the Classground
are far from the marshes of the Nile
where Horus was born on papyrus mats
ducks rising from green paintings

Straight lines and symmetry evoke
the Pharaoh's sacred garden Maru-Aten:
Viewing Place of the God where
leafy beds recalled those holy marshes

Worshippers offered bundles of papyrus
pounded the stalks into flat sheets
for reed pens to record

        the king's accounts
        a bone-setter's text
        a bunch of poems

The lake is missing, worshippers are few
the cemented creek trickles to the river
but a rush of flowers celebrate this air
and the umbrella plant another *Cyperus*
      twirls like a Showground plastic toy

Victoria amazonica

Sydney's Garden has its harbour view
Ballarat its begonias, Melbourne its oak
and Geelong once had a fernery
my great-grandfather built in 1875
but Adelaide was the first where
the Giant Waterlily of the Amazon
would flower

Brought here in the Garden's first year
it failed to bloom until a decade later
they learnt to manage the temperature.
Announced in the city paper
those first pure blossoms
were seen by thirty thousand in a day

Today the pool is almost bare —
only a few lotus leaves remain
the waterlily seeds in clay pots
are still in their special tank
filaments will soon emerge
expand to cover the pool

Leaf buds the size of a fist will uncurl
spread like a giant plate across the water
underleaf struts will strengthen leaves
enough for a child to stand on;
egg shapes unfold to pinkish-white petals
for their short day in the sun

New seed from Guyana will bring vitality
for another century or two

45
*

Mammillaria

Adrian Haworth 1812

Cacti of harsh droughts
        yet the man saw
nourishing nipples

Covered in spines
        yet the man saw
welcoming nipples

Like the *toothed vagina*
        is this a sign of men's
fear-desire ambivalence?

Fine axillary wool
        cushions the spines
masking their threat

Circlets of bright flowers
        encourage risk

Gift of the Goddess

A food powerful enough to sell cars:
Honda means *main rice field*
                    Toyota *rich rice field*
Oryza sativa is a fanciful name
for a staple feeding half the world —
I imagine oryxes and satyrs
                    cavorting in Ortyzia

Placed in Thai caves to feed the dead
                    ten thousand years ago
and brought by the Japanese Sungod
                    from the Fields of Heaven
rice springs from the teeth
        of the Good Genius in China
is offered back in black or purple form
to the Balinese Rice Mother Dewi Sri

Australia came late to its worship
learnt to grow
        sushi and risotto rice
            Kyeema (fragrant rice)
        Doongara (restaurant rice)
Quest (the water-saving rice)
        and Amaroo
            the one most planted

Our Rice Goddess
        is more Kali than Dewi
drinking dry
        the Murrumbidgee
            the Darling and the Murray

Nelumbo Pond

In autumn
even a sacred lotus pond is tatty

Dun-coloured leaves
could be a Thai monarch's sunshade

Domestic mops shake
to reveal opaque brown water

Ducks fuss among the stalks
searching for end-of-year bargains

Two water fowl beep
like river taxis on the Chao Phraya

as they chug past
the centrepiece Boy on a Swan

No longer lost in foliage the cheeky boy
grabs the bird's neck as it strains for flight

Urging it further faster over the water
Under the surface bulbs grow and wait

Fuchsias under the madrona

Was Celia Smedley delicate?
could there have been a Daisy Bell?
Zazz Fifi and Impudence
                        are festive
but was the Abbé Farges so small?

A pink RAF?
a small and pink Soldier of Fortune?
the UFO is open and quite
                        unmysterious

Pinch Me however is
rich folds of velvet
and S'wonderful *is* wonderful

Rose garden

All the lovely and beautiful times we had
All the garlands of violets and roses —
> Sappho

So many rose poems, so many metaphors:
goddess ornament from Artemis to Mary
sign of purity and decadence
pain and passion, love and peace
perfume and healing
      emblem of woman's mystery

In this paddock of excess where to start?
In the Heritage rows with Old Blush
loved for three centuries in the West
or the Romans' favourite I can't find?

Should I describe the unlikely —
the green flowers of *viridiflora*
the domed Snow Carpet
the blue roses the brown *Café*?

Or go to the historical?
Mr Lincoln Gertrude Jekyll Princess Diana
Picasso asking for money
        to have a rose named in his honour

At the Trial Beds a competition has begun
to compare the incomparable
no poem comes:
the roses like good wine need no *bush*

Souvenir de la Malmaison (1843)

A singularly glorious creature
first called Queen of Beauty and Fragrance
       then named by a Russian archduke
for the home of the Empress Josephine
this Bourbon rose of the Chinensis group
the *hundred-petalled* rose
was bred from *Madame Desprez* that
          fairytale heroine who was
     fond of oysters & old wine
     and made coffee to a nicety

These small bushes hardly echo
its history and fame till you're close
       enough to savour
the pale pink of ruffled double flowers
the perfume hinting at spice and the Tropics

I recall that in the Heysen garden at The Cedars
visitors rush to admire the old Malmaison
                    bushes Hans grew from cuttings
he brought from Hahndorf cemetery
now blooming there again on his wife's grave

Nora's early portrait of the rose presents
blooms in four stages: a bud
tightly held by sepals, half-opened buds
the full glory of mature flowers
the translucent loveliness of petals
                    about to fall

In a friend's house beneath the painting
a vase holds blooms grown
                    from Cedars cuttings
perfume envelops the roses
the painting, the viewer

Graffiti

Growing over a metre a day
fifteen hundred varieties used in Japan
a thousand different ways

someone must love bamboo

Seldom in flower then
blooming together dying together
a correspondence humans could envy

New plantings whisper along the path — with
nearby plum and pine 'the three friends of winter'
make a perfect Chinese garden

Stronger gusts and the big canes
beside the creek jostle each other like crowds
in downtown Beijing

the segmented columns a canvas
for hearts and initials in English and Chinese
carefully or casually inscribed

I leave the bamboo untouched
scribble my own challenge to time

The garden of good & evil

Here plants named
for the goddess of love
gobble insects
the Judas tree is also called
the Love Tree

Poisons abound
alongside remedies
deadly nightshade beside
the cure for colic

Leaves cutting like swords
thorns on a bleeding euphorbia
the menace of *Didierea*
the tortured *Pachypodium*
Ferocactus horridus

Ancient cycads like zamia palms prosper
so too the elephant-footed Nolina
and the Mesozoic ginkgo
first tree to evolve and fed
so legend says on milk

Here hundred year old roses grow
with this year's new releases
Imperial chrysanthemums
banana and manioc
date palm and vanilla bean
pyramids of rosemary

A garden for all our seasons

First plant, then build

Cato

Exemplars

Walking along North Terrace
past Florey Mawson Flinders Burns
(such substantial men!)
and a few idealised females — Justice etc
draped around the womanising king

I turn into the Garden and pass
Hebe Diana Venus the Amazon
even modern Andy Goldsworthy
has built a walled black hole

Until behind the historic Morgue I find
a toadstool monument in stone
to Mrs Henry Rymill
Commissioner for Brownies
who took girls from brooms and dishes
to camp under the stars
make shoe racks from twigs

On the rough base the message:
lend a hand   play the game

The brown owl near the toadstool
(Athena's sister) knows this for a beginning

Baying the Sun

the Molossian hounds (copies) 1861

What are Molossian hounds? I ask
         the first classicist I meet
Shakespeare? . . . Theseus? . . .
no, they're Spartan
remembers he rode the statues as a boy
ring me tomorrow

Yes they're from the north of Greece
fierce mastiffs — guard dogs I guess
Lucretius . . . Book Five

These copies are a shiny cream but surely
the Vatican originals were marble
huge dogs with rolypoly necks
         and thickened coats of hair
more domestic than ferocious
or St Bernards without the helpful cask

Their heads roll back and sightless eyes
implore the musician-god Apollo to free them:
guardians of the path to Adelaide's
           most unlikely monument
the dome of ironwork straps and birds
           in Elvis Presley's honour

Amaltheia

Where the Garden began
the temple to Economic Botany
presides over lawn and lake
and the pensive nymph
become downtrodden nanny goat

Nursemaid and saviour of the god
source of the horn of plenty
even her hide became
a heavenly coat for Zeus

What did she get from the godly
encounter?
there's no cornucopia for her
but is that a smile of satisfaction?

The Amazon

In a quiet corner of the Garden
across the lake from *Hebe* and *Diana*
the sun rains gold
on the bare-breasted Amazon
astride her bucking horse
a tiger tearing its neck

Her arm lifts to thrust the lance —
but vandals have taken it
and her gaze misses the tiger
alights on the duckpond

She has ridden here
since the city was new
while her sisters gallop through
Greece and the world's museums
a fear men never quite forget
perhaps a hope

This afternoon
two women sit in the shade
of the solid plinth
talking of herbs and healing

Venus Diana etc

Remarkably incompetent
those ancients:
clutching voluminous robes
to their bosoms
they still expose a nipple
and a breast

Modestly available
their downcast eyes
and submissive pose
men's fantasy

Across the lawn
the bare-breasted Amazon
fights wild beasts
with men's weapons
and wild eyes

She knows the cost
even a breast —
another fantasy?

Flying the flag

In the last years of Queen Victoria
The Pavilion was built
its roof a blue and white helmet
to conjure Kipling and the Punjab

Towards dusk I can see
officers gallop for a chukka or two
between the native Stenocarpus
and an arbutus from North America

The Mediterranean garden keeps its cool

Chapels

How do guests find the right wedding?
three this fine spring Saturday
in just one corner of the Garden

On the shady plane tree lawn
a soprano sings Ave Maria
to her own harp accompaniment
The woman celebrant in muted beige
directs bride and groom in the signing

Behind the Schomburgk Pavilion
an affable priest in snowy robes chats
to crowded guests and wedding party
in the Indian helmet Pavilion.
a string trio plays Pachelbel's canon

Rows of chairs in the Sunken Garden
face a bank of ceanothus and saxifrage
no one yet to play Bach or Mendelssohn
two early guests wander looking lost
they'll be cold by the 4.30 start
when the wind gets up

Wedding photos

Once you paused briefly
on the church steps
while your uncle
pressed the shutter

It's harder now with video:
you have to smile longer
in front of the Rose Garden
with three sisters in bright pink
two pages two flower girls

The photographer decrees
how to hold your head
and when to kiss
directs the scene where
the men carry off the bride
till the sheepish groom
is told to rescue her

On the lawn
the page-boys scuffle
dressed to kill

Coco Indecent

In the Museum of Economic Botany
cases of polished wood hold
the Carpological Collection —

Row after row of seeds and fruits
the small the gross the beautiful
in order of rank in their Kingdom

The tiny, not the immense,
Will teach our groping eyes, the poet said
but my attention goes to big

The bread palm like a pineapple
the sugar pine and jackfruit
the tree-sausage two feet long

No competition for largest —
the immense buttocks of coco de mer
double coconut of the Seychelles

Poet: Francis Webb

weighs eighteen kilos
Lodoiceae maldivica called Coco Indecent
yet *heart-shaped* says the label

Thought to be aphrodisiac
keeping it from the king
cost hands or life

A European ruler paid
forty thousand gold coins
for one nut —

cure for poison and paralysis
more importantly
the Viagra of its day

The Palm House

Straight from the Victorian Age
the glass and decorative iron
      brought from Germany
its elegance only recently restored
it is home to the tortuous survivors
of harsh climates those plants isolated
on Madagascar since Gondwana days

Grey limestone from the Black Forest
stalactites once grown in a cave
now form a grotto with no Madonna
              to adore
though blue flowers at its base make a cross

Too hot to stay for long
in spite of the roof's laser dots
      deflecting the fierce Southern sun
kids run outside to slide down
           the painted rails
play among the Zamia palms

Black Spring

by Andy Goldsworthy

i

Stacked grey biscuits cap a circular wall —
like a Yorkshire sheepfold
           until the wattles grow
the slate comes from Parachilna
but Joe Smith the drystone waller
                is from Scotland

The black of a hole is the flame of a fire —
earth's energy the sculptor says
inside the wall a low slate dome with central hole
antipodean equivalent of
           one he made in Edinburgh
that grey city of bleak castles and John Knox
where sugar blows from the spoon
              before it reaches the cup
This umbilical link through the earth
          could be due for cutting

ii

The weeping wattles have grown
                    to enfold the stones —
Black Spring is more at home

Seen from the path behind
it could be an outback tank stand
                    without its windmill

The umbilical link to Scotland is still there
perhaps the tide now flows the other way

No wind no rain

During Artists' Week
people-sized weather stations
have appeared on the rise
of the Araucaria Avenue

roofless and lined with Buddhist
symbols — the question mark
the exclamation point —
these stilted boxes invite me in

limit my sight to sky and sign
encourage me to listen
to explore less and more
focus on the weather of my mind

Conservatory

A wheel full-circle —
the Garden gave the Zoo its first animals
now the Zoo sends birds back
to the Bicentennial Conservatory
that teepee of glass towering
over tree shrub and sculpture

A thousand jets in the roof make
a rainforest for tropic plants and
                    bugs and birds
even in summer children love to race
along the winding paths and boardwalks
                at treetop height
as their sweating parents wait below

White-browed woodswallows
                    dart through green fronds
of King Fern Pandanus Giant Fishtail Palm
and startled visitors on the boardwalk
            to catch the palm-destroying moths
useful busy so visible

Two Noisy Pittas hide
their confection of colours on the leafy floor
quiet and unseen these *jewel thrushes* hop
                              within metres of visitors
until sunlight catches gems of yellow
                                    and turquoise
mate-less in spring both males build nests
whistle their hopeful call:
perhaps the females in the Zoo across the Park
                        will hear and come

Cascade

by Sergio Redegalli

Sphinx from one side, yak from another
thin sheets of glass so lightly tinted green
form an arch above the shallow pool
Quiet cascades

Everything is mirrored
the path and lawn
the Judas tree
I too am visible

Through the arch of blue-green panes
I read a sign from
the new rain forest conservatory:
What of the Future?

Uncertain of tomorrow for planet or me
I choose the path through tall trees
drop my mandarin peel in the bin

Notes

These poems, written over several years, occasionally refer to features and plants now gone. I have included them since part of a garden's charm is the way it changes and grows over time. The cages have gone from the Wollami pines and there are now no fuchsias under the Madrona, and no Madrona. Rhododendron *Sappho* is dead.

p 14 Hallam, Lord Tennyson, was Governor of South Australia and later Governor General of Australia. He was the first child of the poet who named him after his great friend Arthur Henry Hallam, for whom he wrote the elegy, In Memoriam.

p 35 The proverb, Good wine needs no bush, goes back to Roman times when ivy bushes (sacred to Bacchus) were used to advertise taverns and wine sellers.

p.39. 'The trio of pine, plum and bamboo,
known as the three friends of winter, was
indispensable in a Chinese garden.'
Richard Aitken: Botanical Riches.

p. 50 The poet was Francis Webb.

Some of these poems have been published in *Adelaide
Review*, *FourW*, *Otis Rush*, *Southerly*, *Tarantella*, the
anthology *Hope & Fear*, and in *sun wind & diesel*.

Acknowledgements

My thanks are due to many workers and volunteers in the Garden who over the years have answered my queries. Thekla Reichstein and latterly, Laine Langridge gave much support.

Special thanks also to Sophie Abbott for the use of her lotus photographs for the cover. As usual, my writing group and Ruth Raintree have given me so much.

Also by Miriel Lenore
and available from Wakefield Press

sun wind & diesel

ISBN 978 1 86254 419 2

drums & bonnets

ISBN 978 1 86254 628 8

the Dog Rock

ISBN 978 1 86254 666 0

For more information visit
www.wakefieldpress.com.au

Wakefield Press is an independent publishing and
distribution company based in Adelaide, South Australia.
We love good stories and publish beautiful books.
To see our full range of titles, please visit our website at
www.wakefieldpress.com.au.